"So, if you're tired to speak,

sit next to me.

For I too, am fluent in silence."

R. Arnold

Sweet

Self

Destruction

Mariana Prado

Disclaimer:

This is nothing but a conglomeration of the simple feelings of a complex individual, some of them good, some of them less so. This is nothing but my way of communicating my history and my truth.

The poems do not linearly correspond with the events of my lifetime; I have realigned them for aesthetic purposes. I can guarantee that you will relate with at least one of the feelings explored in the pages that follow.

From the depths of my heart, I hope that these words can touch you, like I was once touched by someone else's poetry. I hope they will bring you joy, a sense of shared humanity, or even tears, if that is what you need at the moment.

I would like to dedicate this debut (hoping there will be more to come) to someone who never read or even mentioned poetry to me, but showed me poetry in the forms of love, music, understanding and forgiveness. He was always proud of me, no matter what; always bragging loudly about my small accomplishments.

Dad, you were an example to be followed, the most luminous individual I have ever had the pleasure of knowing. I am sorry I could not be there for you in the end, but I know your love is immortal. It will always be with me.

So now, for some Sweet Self Destruction.

Enjoy!

The beginning

"In the beginning was the Word, and the Word was with God, and the Word was God."

John 1:1

I mean no harm when I write about pain.

I mean no bad when I made you part of my poetry.

And I seek nothing but beauty when I kill you with my words.

1 - Inspiration

I read your book

and, for a moment,

I heard your voice,

felt your pain and thought of you.

I read your words as someone

who sings a prayer.

In your face,

I saw myself as a mirror

I wanted to be inside your heart

to understand you better.

as part of your flesh

what fate gave you.

But as I'm still me

and I can't dress myself as you.

I made me similar

and mirrored my words on yours.

With my knees on the floor

and my spirit in my hands.

I wrote my own poetry and dreamt.

Dreamt of a day

you might read my words.

hear my voice.

feel my pain and think of me.

I dreamt of a moment

where you might also

wish to live inside my heart.

And only this way,

the circle would be closed.

You gave voice to my soul -

thank you!

(To Rupi Kaur)

2

Wishful Thinking
(To V)

One day,

on a humid summer morning,

when the warmth of the sun

touches your skin lightly

while you are still in bed.

You'll be rolling around in your

sheets,

not wanting to get up

and expecting nothing from the world.

You'll think of me.

You will remember how easy

it was for my hands,

when over your body,

to bring you right up to fire and lust,

and also down to sleep and slumber.

You'll think of my fingertips,

sliding across your hair,

lightly stroking your palms,

in those moments when we were

in between the reign of dreams

and the ecstasy freshly felt.

And you will miss me.

You'll miss my tongue;

you'll miss the way my warm lips

planted the most lascivious kisses

over your whole being.

~~How bent~~ my body would go

for your pleasure

and how divinely passionate

I would let everything else unfold.

To simply shiver and die in your arms.

under your spell.

Eyes and skin in flames.

You will think of the nights with no

end. the bright colours exploding

in bliss and my low voice

begging for more.

even when I couldn't bear it anymore

and yet felt greedy.

You'll remember the shape of my waist

when you held it tight.

and the rhythmic shake of my hips

on top of you.

Your mouth will water when you

remember my scent and my taste.

and the silk of my hair

brushing over your face.

Your skin will shiver and you'll know

I'll always be there.

invading your dreams.

tormenting your thoughts.

Stuck in your sweat.

imprinted on your surface.

no matter how many times you wash it.

Like an under-skin tattoo,

attached to your bone marrow.

You will know that there is no escape,

there is no end and the memory

of what I am

will always be there,

as something immortal and intangible.

You'll always remember me!

3

You kissed my lips

and your hands held my waist

softly

you pulled my body closer

without making any promises;

but your eyes did.

I looked at you sleeping

and wished you stayed more

touched me more.

loved me more.

Yet you broke my heart.

Or what was left of it.

What now?

I ask.

Now nothing.

I'm going to kiss somebody else's lips

and pull their waists.

I'm going to hold them softly.

make promises I won't keep

and break their hearts.

Because now

everyone is you.

and I need to share

what you gave me.

Pain that

Spreads!

4

A love letter

This is not another poem.

trying to hide the ugly truth

behind beautiful metaphors.

This is maybe.

a love letter to all that was lost.

sad and misunderstood.

To all lovers in the past

I no longer remember the touch

To all friends in the past

I no longer remember the laugh

To the loved ones who have passed.

To all regrets and bad decisions

that brought us here, right now

To all lost nights we, in vain,

tried to fix unfixable mistakes.

To the waste of time,

to the waste of energy

and to the worry.

Let us celebrate

what was normal and unnecessary,

yet precious.

A love letter to all apologies

we let die in our chests,

and couldn't get out

Maybe for fear.
maybe for pride.
To all soured relationships
buried in that blue spot
in the corner of our hearts.
To abandoned feelings and hopes
we forget to feed.
so they just dry out
and get forgotten.
To all the forgotten ones.

to all messages, with no answers

and calls we were meant to give,

but never did.

To those ones waiting

on the other side for our calls.

To overthinking and lost causes,

a love letter to the outsiders

and bullied ones.

to time lost in sweet futilities

and stupid ideas.

To unhealthy relationships
we all had in the past,
now long gone.
To the lack of common sense
and loneliness.
to the lone wolves.
I want to celebrate
our humanity as individuals
and our tears in the shower.

Let us celebrate our flaws
and the beauty of being imperfect,
organic and impure.
Let me write this love letter
to all breaths lost in bed,
to sweaty sheets,
to meaningless encounters
and frivolous pleasures
we enjoy so much.

To nights with no stars.

to the owls' hooting

and the perfection of the darkness.

Finally the darkness.

my most misunderstood friend

who has always embraced me

when I need to sleep.

rest and dream.

And to all the dreamers,

restless

or asleep,

around me.

5

Come again

Please.

I crave your touch.

I crave your lips on my skin.

burning like a hot iron

marking me for life.

Please.

come again.

don't leave me here hanging

while this desire burns my insides.

consumes me

and melts my core.

You took my spirit

and my body

now lies empty.

walking in slow motion.

black and white in the crowd.

Please.

I am thirsty for your sweat

dripping on my face.

dancing down your neck

to my tongue.

I am hungry for the nourishment

you gave my soul.

for the hours in that time vortex

we used to lose ourselves in.

I need to feel the hot flames

of your hands

and your mouth opening to me again.

Please.

come again.

Please. come again to me.

6

There's always uncertainty

in your gestures.

Confusing stares.

half smiles.

You don't love me

but maybe you want me.

I don't love you.

but I certainly need you.

The tension in the air is palpable.

I dance,

your eyes dance with me.

I smile,

your eyes smile with me.

Your hands shake around,

my waist waits for them.

You talk,

my lips shiver for a spell.

Our minds tell us we shouldn't,

our bodies disagree.

7

She

I don't know why I call her "she"

maybe that's my way

of giving her a face.

maybe that's my way

of giving her a weakness.

because sometimes

it feels like she owns me.

She has the hold of my strength,
keeping it tight, small,
squeezed under her feet.
She has the power
to bring all the clouds
of endless tears
to cover my sun,
keeping me in darkness.
She feeds from my pain
and grows from my misery.

She tells me how ugly I am.

how unworthy of love I am.

and why I have been so alone —

because that's what I deserve.

and that's where I'm supposed to be.

And I believe her.

I can't see properly.

my vision is blurred

and my skin is frozen.

It's like being naked. alone
in a cold. dark box.
Looking from here
everything seems dead.
everything seems empty.
my voice is gone.
I try to look around for any help
but all I see
are the life-threatening things
calling out my name.

8

Blue

(To R)

I found myself submerged

in the pool of your eyes

Your lips move.

and your perfect teeth show off.

I have no idea

what you're talking about

because the colour of your skin

makes my thoughts sink.

I am drowning.

Drowning in the strong

sound of your voice.

drowning in the heat

your words light up in me.

I touch your face lightly.

with the tips of my fingers.

and the silky texture

of your beard gives me chills;

they come up my spine in waves.

electricity

bringing me closer and closer

to you.

deeper and deeper

into your presence.

The smell of your neck

is hypnotic

and puts me in a trance.

So I dance free.

feeling your kind eyes surround me.

feeling the energy of your soul

and your soothing aura

slowly enveloping

the room.

The kind of thing you feel.

but can't name.

The kind of thing you know.

but can't understand.

Your left profound marks

under my skin

behind my eyes

and in the back of my

head.

and now you're part of me.

9

Inner turbulence

My thoughts feel

like a messy storm —

noisy, constrictive.

All of the facts,

all of the words

all of the images

I can't let any of them go,

can't forget a single syllable.

His words.

her acts.

your thoughts.

my life

being held in other people's hands.

Can't let go.

my brain shakes

my spirit fights.

overwhelmed.

The anxiety,

the anguish,

all the anger.

Sadness is not strong enough

of a word.

What I feel is deeper,

darker,

somewhere between hell

and my own perception of limbo.

Somebody look at me —

somebody help.

please!

Nobody listens to the empty voice

stuck in my chest.

Every minute this torment goes on,

I die a little.

10

I wish

I wish you were mine.

so I'd know where your hands lie

before your last thought at night.

I wish you were mine

so I could have you

within my embrace

every day before we arise.

I wish your eyes belonged to me.
so I could show you my brightness.
the stars of my heart.
I wish you'd see me
in the same light I see you.
so we could shine in darkness of life
together.
You are a blaze
in a sad and scary night.

Your eyes guide my feet like torches,

leading me through the confusion

of the crowd.

Your arms are blankets

for my cold, damp skin.

Your kisses are death and resurrection,

softness and hard ice,

burning me from the inside,

cremating my feelings.

I wish you were mine

so I could rest from this agony

that is living without you.

11

Come

Come to me and tell me
you were undeniably wrong.
Come and tell me all the rudeness
and indifference was fear.
Come and say how afraid you are
and submit to me the depth of your
feelings.

Come,

just come!

Storm into the room, with your eyes,

your heart and your arms wide open.

Come and say how much you want me

and how precious all of this is.

Come and bring your smell,

your nudity

and all the fullness of your being.

Come with your paleness,

your muscles

and the mess of your feelings.

Come with all your lies,

phobias and weaknesses.

Just come,

come and take me away

from this inertia.

Come and love me how I do.

come to me with your body.

your mind and your soul.

And when you come.

come naked.

invigorated.

come free.

But just come to me.

12

Yin and yang
(To B and S)

They are yin and yang

black and white.

glowing in the dark

before my eyes.

They complete me

as the puzzle my body is.

She is the smell of coconuts.

a scent coming from the sea

in a tropical paradise.

Dark skin. dark light.

a sky with no stars.

creamy chocolate

melting under my tongue.

Soft as candy floss

and just as sweet.

He shines like the blue skies

of a summer morning,

Golden like the sun,

burning my skin

with his lips and hands.

Scratching my face

with his silky beard,

making me lose my senses

somewhere between life and death.

They complete me, yin and yang.

Braids and blonde hair.

blues eyes and ebony skin.

softness.

gratitude in the form of breathing.

connection in the form of sweat.

life in the form of rhythm

Polyamory can be real

13

What should we do
when we no longer wish to be?
What should we do
when our own weight
is just too much to carry?
How to escape yourself
when you just can't stand
your own face in the mirror?
How to keep walking

when every step feels

like nails are being pinned

on your soles?

Just breathe!

- They say -

So we keep on breathing.

And our wish to vanish

remains harboured. firmly.

We push on.

detesting the face in the mirror,

carrying a burden we cannot bear

and feeling those nails

stuck in our skin

endlessly.

We bleed and nobody sees

She's always around

14

Stockholm Syndrome

We learn to live in cages,

giving affection to our captors,

afraid of losing a love

that was never there.

You were a parasite

feeding from my weakness,

sucking up my spirit.

draining my soul.

taking life from my veins.

And I let you –

I allowed your cruelty.

your heavy words.

The weight of being.

existing was too much.

But then I left

And I could breathe, again,
feel my own back, again.
Once more,
my feet touched the ground
and I was still alive.
I was myself, again,
learning anew.

trying to free my heart

from the ghost of that trap.

For all the Gods above us,

we should never learn

to live in cages,

or give love to our captors.

(The ex fiancée)

15

Nosebleed

I have learned to love myself

with the same violence

I once used to seek self-destruction.

and I'll defend with ferocity

what I once endangered so effortlessly.

So do not touch my soul with dirty

hands.

and don't kiss my heart if your lips'
intentions aren't pure.
I've decided that I'm no longer
available to bleed for others
or to let little crumbs lure me into cages
of selfishness and self-doubt.
I no longer can be fooled with vain
promises or dreams made of paper.
So if you want to see my naked spirit,
be prepared to undress your own.

(Inner Truth)

16

Friendzoned

Why won't you look at me?

Well, you do,

but you can't see me.

I am hanging here,

always around

with my arms wide open

with my heart exposed

yet you won't see me.

I project my wishes over you.

my dreams.

desires.

I know you can sense them.

yet you won't see me.

My love is such a potent thing.

overflowing.

Others feel its pull. its traction.

They dance for me,
they stare at me,
they try and drink from it
and sometimes it is so much
I can't help sharing it
with someone else.
And yet... you won't see me.
It's all over my eyes
when we dance
and look at each other.

It is in the layer of sweat in my skin

when you simply touch me

without seeing me.

It's sad how I long for your touch,

your hands and lips,

and you won't see me.

(First love)

17

There are dark purple flowers

growing in a small garden

at the back of my head.

They are soft

and smell like cotton candy ice cream

in a summer twilight.

so I know

there is always perfume in me.

There are goldfish

swimming in the waterline

of my eyes.

Sometimes they blur my vision

and make me see things

that are not there.

so I know fantasy exists within me.

I have a pack of wild wolves

running between my thighs.

They howl to the full moon

and enrol me in mischief all too often.

I am clearly innocent,

but I smirk to myself

So I am assured that my passion

runs strong.

I have a den
of red and orange snakes
encircling my waist,
they are venomous,
but they keep my skin protected
against the predators
I bring upon myself.
They are patient and forgiving,
but strike out with fury when provoked.
So I know, in my core, I am safe.

There is a contemplative little owl,

nesting on the left side of my chest.

She doesn't do much,

but her presence keeps me at peace

and balance.

Without her,

I wouldn't be myself.

So I know

there's some wisdom

in me.

Others never notice them,

but starfish live tangled

in the strands of my hair,

bringing the salty smell of the ocean

to my days,

as they sing

the high tide songs to me.

So I know there will always be music

around.

There are some rose thorns

curled up around my neck.

They don't often sting,

but they are there to remind me

of the hard times,

to be vigilant, always

of what might come back one day.

So I know sadness will forever

be part of me, too.

Little blue butterflies

swing their wings

inside the capillaries of my wrists,

tickling me,

making me giggle out of the blue.

So I know there is joy,

just at the reach of my hands.

And on the tip of my right foot,

there has always lived a firefly,

although it took me forever

to recognise its presence.

Its light is blue, pure and soothing,

aiding me in moments of uncertainty,

guiding my steps.

Now I know there is always light in

me.

Always.

18

A song to what was, what wasn't
and what it could have been
(To V)

There was something intrinsically pure

in the way you so often made me die

and come back to life

completely submerged in pleasure.

On all those nights we shared in

absolute oblivion.

all the touches and heavy breaths

I'll crave for quite some time

after the end

Also the way my screaming mind

managed to shut itself up

when you were there.

I guess one can dream of silence.

even if that dream is way too farfetched

I often think of how paradoxical

it was.

that in the midst of my dread

to share my sheets.

I found my voice insisting

for you to stay.

for nights with no end.

The peace that came with your presence

was worth the discomfort

of having other feet touching mine.

You think I kept coming back

for some strong body feature

you may possess.

some others think I stayed

because you have the prettiest of skins.

or the perfect touch when we got mixed

up in each other's sweat.

Of course they all mattered after all.

but I stayed because of what's within;

the hypnotic kindness of your eyes.

how your boyish smile

used to light up the room.

like the sun on a summer morning.

And how they made me believe in

non- existent fairy tales.

They made my legs tremble every time.

they made me fool myself that maybe.

maybe I could live

in those tales.

But that world can't be inhabited.

doors are shut

and there is nothing I can do.

Sadly!

I could have shown you

all the ingrown love

I have residing inside my heart.

Never used for real before.

as pure as the death

also living on its side.

Both dormant for now.

latter that you could

so easily see

Latent care that I tried to.

so desperately share.

through my hugs and kisses.

Untouched it is.

Untouched it will remain

And I am resigned.

resigned to the fact we got

those rare moments.

glad that we had the opportunity

to climb each other's minds

and find some solace for so long.

And I'm sure I can keep

some of that alive in me.

Maybe this part of you

will always remain.

like a sanctuary I can always revisit

for sweet memories and kind nostalgia.

So I will always praise those nights.

19

Made of glass

Your skin is now
made of glass.
I can see
through your flesh and blood
the heartbeat of someone who suffers.
You feel the weight of the stars
on your tired shoulders

and a river of a thousand tears

flooding your quintessence.

There is sorrow on the floor

spread under your shoes,

grabbing at your ankles

like poisoned vines.

They follow your footsteps

through the hours of your life.

It's all about them...

They left you.

they abused you.

they hurt you.

They didn't care about your wounds.

They broke your glass skin.

And now you cry and bleed.

cracked in pieces, you grieve

lying on the wet red soil.

I can see melancholy

hovering above your head.

dragging down your spirit

like an anchor.

And so. I ask you

what now. glass skin?

Are you going to lie there?

Just waiting for the rain

to take your pieces away?

Won't you try and find that fix

to rebuild yourself whole?
Will you keep crying
and pretending
you're not alive anymore?
I am here,
just watching.
Just waiting, glass skin.

Waiting for you
to turn that glass
into unbreakable crystal.
To finally shine.

Looking in the mirror

20

The tip of your tongue

the tip of my breast

the tip of your fingers

the tip of the part of me

that only I know best.

You touch me.

Softly.

With the tip of your fingers

Coming up my legs

Burning up my skin

you hold me.

on the top of your legs.

Pushing.

Positioning.

reducing the space between us.

You get me.

Your eyes find mine.

our breaths in sync.

We're just one thing

moving slow. soft. hard.

fast...

Then slow again.

Your smell takes over the air,

your noises take over my thoughts.

I'm nothing but part of you.

You're nothing but part of me.

We're nothing.

We're everything.

Soon you leave me, too soon —

so brief.

just a second in space.

I already miss you.

the tip of your tongue.

the tip of your fingers.

the top of your thighs.

A hook up

21

There is no sadness

in the dark and cold of winter.

It is my home, my safe harbour.

The sadness lies

in the glimpse of spring.

When the sunlight

and the colour of the flowers

Bring the promise of a happiness

that might not come.

22

Running with scissors

My feet have always been addicted

to find its way through hard

and rough paths.

even when my mind knew those ways

were not the ones for me to take.

But they were the prettiest.

I've always thought.

Trying to silver line the pain

caused by the sharp blades and
prickles sank into my ankle's skin.
I always had this tendency
of simply ignoring the pain.
when there is something sparkly
and shiny to be admired.
And I don't know any other way...
I knew from the moment my hands
touched your burning golden skin.

those dreams weren't made

for me to have.

But I still had them

and now I see the glass ceiling

shattering above my head

while I stand, inert, looking up.

Just waiting for the powdered crystal

to blind my hopes again.

I certainly had it coming and yet

here I am.

staring surprised while the world

falls apart and slips through my tired

and bleeding fingers.

I know I bring hell into my heart

on purpose.

and I don't know any other way...

But I did have some faith.

I truly did.

Not because you had the prettiest
of the feathers.
nor because your singing was the softest
I could hear for so long.
It wasn't because you brought honeyed
paradise with your tongue and
fingertips.
No. it was for the fact you planted
silence into the deafening noise inside
my head.

that maybe this one time

things would be different.

What a fool I am!

It wasn't. it never is. it never will be

I fly too close to the sun far too often.

I burn my wings and cripple

my hopes far too much.

that I've became almost completely

numb on the surface.

But I don't know any other way...

Then my spirit comes out

missing a slice every time

I try to venture into somebody's arms,

knowing those arms could be

sharp blades just waiting

to cut my love in half.

And here I am,

missing so much inside

that my core is almost hollow, a void.

Lost in the depths of the sorrows

I inflicted myself.

An open heart, open wound,

exposed and pulsing,

Craving what I never had

in the first place.

But I don't know any other way.

23

There was magic in my body

making me dance around your figure.

You pulled me,

you led me

as colours sparkled

in the lights above us

and powdered happiness

circulated in my blood.

We stopped for a moment.

and for that moment our lips touched.

Soft and warm you were,

small and protected I felt.

My spirit floated for a brief instant

and met yours inside our mouths.

My breath was heavy

my heart grew bigger.

rumbling strong under my chest.

Pleasure.

such intense pleasure!

I felt my soul inside your body.

our souls dancing

connected around us.

Together we were.

one thing we were.

There was so much light

in your tongue.

so much purity in your thoughts.

so much beauty in your heart.

I wanted to live there forever

and when I left

a cracked part of me stayed

forever buried inside of your core.

forever lost within your spirit.

Now I'm lying here

with a broken soul

missing a piece

you took away forever.

Out of body experience

(to R at TG)

24

Obsession

Your voice echoes in my mind

as a prayer

repeatedly. over and over

I hear the sounds you make

when you love.

mixed with the words of no more –

I don't love you

never would

never will.

I want you like a forbidden fruit

Knowing I can't have it

I dream of your smell

and wake up sweaty.

craving your heavy hands

on my breasts.

I don't love you —

never would.

never will.

Yet you're like a virus

stuck in my body.

Your imprint won't let go,

my obsessive mind won't let go

My turbulent desire

is a reflex of futility.

Raw passion of a night.

Envy of something

I can never possess.

My emptiness forever unfulfilled.

I don't love you.

never would.

never will.

25

Agent of chaos

When the liquid light of that cold
morning touched your winter eyes and
the snow white of your smile made my
stomach twist for the first time.
I've realised how easy it is for me to
walk straight into the eye of the
hurricane.
How I invite war into my chest

and how, without even blinking,

I bring all have into a broken glass

storm and smile...

Every. Fucking. Time.

I am deeply, irrevocably in trouble.

I always am, maybe always will be.

And maybe there is some beauty

in the fact that my heart can't find

peace when I am at peace.

It finds solace in chaos

and mayhem is where
I always called home;
So make no mistake
to think things are going well.
They never are.
So no, my dear.
This love doesn't have to see the broad
day light and sunshine doesn't need to
touch its face.
It's better if stays unspoken.
Inhabiting the mist.

Like the idea of inspiration that lives
just in my mind, and doesn't really
have the intention of becoming
something real.
Like a seed, planted in darkness,
which brings in its core the smell of
the flowers it could have become.
But won't.
Don't hate me for walking away,
my love.

I am done not being what others want.

All the rivers that I cried are

flowing back into my eyes,

all the prayers I have sang to the

Gods are now coming back to my core

as music played by the stars.

Touching my bones, rearranging them

back in order and I don't need any of

this anymore.

I think I never did,

but didn't know that.

Don't think I am sad or in pain,

after you ate my pride,

this all became normal, homely.

Feels like I'm back into my mother's

womb. Not even that toxic.

Happiness made a promise to never

share a room with me again.

we have broken up so early in life

I can barely remember its face.

So now I can only thrive in anarchy

and turmoil. So don't feel sorry for me.

Don't let all the inconsistencies

confuse you.

they are all my dear close friends.

And in their hands

I lie and fly away.

26

Slowly (To C)

Slowly, my heart gets rid of you.

Slowly, I forget you

and my body gets some rest.

Slowly, the shape of your face
falls apart in my memory
and slowly the marks
you left on my skin fade.
Slowly, I stop thinking
remembering
crying.
slowly my love dies
and desire disappears.

leaving behind just the bitterness

of your dead cold heart

in the back of my tongue.

Slowly.

the heavy words are worth more

than the promised love ones.

and slowly you go forever.

Slowly the memory of your lips

becomes a distant image

fading in the past.

Slowly you become of the past

and this past becomes dead history

forgotten in an old album

of a dead social media.

27

Don't go looking around

in the empty light of a dead star

for a love who does not live there.

Don't go forcing your heart

to walk barefoot

on a cold and damp floor.

when it could be held

and carried by warm,

soft hands.

Don't go chasing those feelings

we knit alone at night.

rolling around in an empty bed.

suffocating our peace

in tears of loneliness.

Don't love what tires you.

what you have to pull by the arm

to make yourself seen.

No – don't think you have to suffer
to have what should be given
with an open heart and a soft smile.
Recalculate what doesn't want
to be on your route
and let fly what doesn't want to stay.
Focus on what does.
Let go of the Frankenstein of dead
hopes.

and free your thoughts

from empty promises.

You will need your breath

for uncontrollable laughs

and the buzz of the butterflies within.

Free yourself from the scars

of the past —

your skin will need space

for soft and caring fingers

or firm and strong ones,

if that's what you like!

But most importantly,

free your spirit from the weight

of the wrong lovers in your past.

There's new sun to be felt

just around the corner.

Before you find your soulmate

You need to find yourself.

28

I will love you (To S)

No matter how distant

your physical body might be.

I will love you.

No matter how far away

your mind and your thoughts

may dwell.

I will love you.

No matter how hard it is

when sometimes you throw stones at me

and cast me out of paradise,

I still love you.

I don't care if you push me away

and retire from my presence.

I don't care if you cut my skin

and break my bones.

I will love you.

I'd pluck my eyes out.

so you can see.

I'd rip my chest open.

so you can have a beating heart

and feel

that I love you.

Even when the figure of your face

is just a distant shadow fading.

a small flame dying from my memory.

I will know

that deep down

hidden somewhere among

the pieces of my mourning soul

I will love you.

I will always love you.

A friendship ends,

real love never does

29

There were so many words unsaid.

so many feelings left behind

abandoned like old rags with no use.

You gave me no choice but resentment

the shape of which is wrong

for my heart.

It doesn't fit there.

its sharp corners make me bleed.

I wish we had more time.

I wish we had more courage

to be brave enough

and face the truth.

We're both broken.

perhaps unfixable.

Maybe not –

maybe you're just another idiot.

Too coward to give in.

too scared to love

30

Some days, when the floor is unstable

and you look up at the skies,

you see the stars have left you.

Light has left you.

All you see is the dark.

Now you're not looking up anymore

because darkness has spread inside,

and raising your eyes again is hard.

raising your body
from the sheets even harder.
She has returned. she
with her eternally wet eyes.
cold hands
and cruel words.
Now small things have overgrown.
pithy struggles can kill
and you're there in the pit again.

You worked so hard

to not fall back in

but it was no use.

You're there —

you need to take back your control.

you need to take back your soul.

that got lost in the same depths

your self-esteem crawls.

Go get them.

We need them.

Grab the love you forgot you had.

hold on tight.

Put it together with the strength

you thought had died – it has not.

Look the important ones in the eye.

show them your tears.

let them hug you.

Let their hugs put together
the broken pieces of your spirit.
Let them say everything will be fine.
and believe it!
Please. don't give up!
Please. don't give up!

To all the sad ones. To myself.

31

I'm not looking for a new love

I'm not looking for a new love.
but if I were
I'd expect him to have
the gentle touch of carnation petals
in the tip of his fingers.
So that when he caresses me

I'd only feel the exquisite
sensation of warm flowers
sliding across my skin.

I'm not looking for a new love.
but if I were
I'd like her to have
the bright white light of the new moon
reflecting on her teeth.
so that her smile would guide me

through the darkness of my own

loneliness.

I'm not looking for a new love,

but if I were

I'd like him to have

a golden fount of honey

dripping down

from the corner of his lips

so I could drink the sweetness

and get rid of the bitter taste

past lovers left behind.

I'm not looking for a new love.

but if I were

I'd like you to have

a little spark brought from the sun

in your eyes.

so that when you look at me

you would illuminate

the perished parts of my heart
that's still too stubborn to give in.
Bringing it back to life.
Giving it back to me.

32

You are

Your skin is like the forbidden fruit

Eve found in paradise.

pure sin.

Your hands are like

the hottest magma

ascending a volcano.

pure fire.

Your lips are like the softest music

played by Vivaldi.

pure art.

Your hair is like sunbeams

reflected in a glass.

pure light.

You're sin, fire, art and light.

When you share the music

 in your eyes,

the poetry in your breath

and the sugar of your spirit,

my soul swims deep in pleasure,

drowning itself in happiness.

You're happiness

and the medicine for my ills.

33

I saw your eyes for the last time
yesterday. in a dream.
Your expression was kind
and your wrinkles had gone away.
You smiled for a brief instant.
then said goodbye with a gesture.
Those eyes spoke to me.
Don't fight it. they said.

The leaves fall.

the waters run.

the fire burns.

And life is fluid.

My existence slipped

through your fingers

like a liquid you tried to drink

and none of this is our fault.

Feel the pain.

the burn in your chest.

I am here for you.

I always have been,

always will.

even if it's just a distant image.

Love can't die.

Don't fight it.

Let it burn, let it run... Let it fall.

None of it is under our control.

so just feel it.

Let the tears clear your face,

let the pain settle.

Move on.

I miss you, dad. Every day.

34

One day you looked at me

with your empty eyes,

your empty heart

and your empty words.

I looked back at you

and your empty promises

sounded different.

The emptiness you left in my life.

in my childhood.

in my soul —

now was clear.

I saw the void you left in my chest.

the destructive power you have

within veins.

and I stopped believing you.

I stopped crying at your absence.

I stopped mourning your negligence.

I stopped missing what

you could never give

because you simply didn't possess it.

I found love within myself.

I found forgiveness

deep down in my spirit.

The resentment is gone.

so is the sadness

so are the tears

and so are the empty hopes.

I do not hate you
but I cannot love you.
Trauma does not simply go away
but the wound no longer hurts.
I wish you could be happy
but I won't be there.
You are a need
I no longer have,
and for that
I couldn't be more grateful.

To the absent narcissist mother.

35

Performing miracles from despair

I sew a thread joining back

the cracked pieces of my soul

calmly.

I put together the jigsaw puzzle

that my heart became

and breathe...

I contemplate my own reflection

in the looking glass.

The face staring back

is not the one I once knew.

Tears have left

profound marks on my cheeks.

staining the skin

damaging the smile.

I can still see the long-gone

black-eyed girl staring back.

and for a second

when I close my eyes

I can feel her gaze upon our life.

Together we defeated dragons.

teared down castles.

prisons and towers.

They abandoned us. abused us.

they disfigured our hopes

and crushed our spirit.

We failed and fell.

we cried and gave up

We have died so many times

And yet. here we are

I can feel her fingertips

stroking my skin.

her hands are warm and soothing.

They bring new beams of hope

traveling through the surfaces

of my body.

I can breathe new strength.

She stretches out to the starry night.

and uses the moon to tie my hair.

its bright white light

pulses in my insides

telling me she's sorry.

she's terribly sorry.

The black cloak of the night
envelops me
as the black-eyed girl
cleanses my face
and plants a kiss on my forehead.
I know there's healing there
I understand there's peace inside
I learn it all comes from within.
The darkness is my refuge
where I can sleep and rest.

The midnight moon is the maiden

hugging my fears.

putting the broken pieces

back in the right place.

telling me with her musical voice

we can perform miracles from despair.

Every day.

36

Pretend (to M)

Look at me in the eye

and pretend I was there.

Pretend I was always there for you

in the moments you felt most alone.

Pretend I was there when

you hid yourself in the closet and cried.

You thought nobody was looking.

so you counted your tears

and stocked them in a box full of dust.

Pretend!

Pretend I was there

cradling your head.

cuddling your darkness

and breastfeeding your hopes.

When your soul tried so desperately

to crawl out of those shadows.

Please, pretend the bones

holding my heart in place

were not broken,

from trying to breathe so painfully

among the smoke

my spirit used to exhale.

Pretend we were happy,

when that love felt like the only thing

preventing us from falling

into the dark pits

of our own bitter cravings.

Pretend that was the only thing

feeding me and nurturing my flesh.

When the air felt like

stones being transported

by the tiny veins of my throat

just to ensure the beats of my heart

continue.

Pretend you loved me,

pretend I loved you.

Not because we were hopeless

or lonely like the morning star

in a winter dawn.

Pretend you cared once,

even when you watched me

dream from afar

and stepped aside, enraged,

impatient with my childish desires.

Pretend my acts were not cruel when
I left.
when I couldn't carry on
living in that dull domain.
Pretend we were not damaged
 intoxicating each other with our venom
floating around like lost kites.
Pretend we were happy and content.
and from our bliss.

a modest flower grew

with white little spots of light.

illuminating with candid beams

the sombre caves of our existence.

To the sad musician

37

You walk through the golden
paths of existence
just to look back and realise that
you can't make people love you.
no matter how much of it you have
urgently overflowing your core —
you can't make them love you.

You can have all the understanding
amongst the stars in the Cosmos
of the strength of your feeling.
You can be so sure
of the healing properties.
If your fingertips
ever touch their spirit.
but you can't make them love you.

They can be blind. drunk.

naked in the dark.

They can be lost. alone.

in pain within their frozen skin.

but you can't make them love you.

You can look in the future.

see the happiness and joy.

bliss and ecstasy

swirling around your blazing souls.

but you can't make them love you.

You can emerge

from the centre of the bonfire

dressed in a lava satin skirt.

twirling among the flames, smiling.

burning down the pain

some cold soul left behind.

crawling in those fields —

and yet

you can't make them love you.

What you can do is —

put on those storm shoes

I know you have.

light up the volcano

trapped between those ribs.

embrace the chaos

living within your breasts

and dance.

Dance to the music

of your heartbeats.

dance till the end of times

when only the Gods can see.

And smile.

smile and forget about them

because you don't need them.

not like they need you.

38

I want to show you my flames,
the ardent ambers I carry
on my lips and fingertips.
I want to melt your body
into the inferno
I have stuck inside my ribs.
I want to turn your cold winter eyes
into red searing lava

that I can drink from.

choke on.

die of.

I want to watch my fire

devouring your spirit.

consuming your flesh

from inside out.

Coming off your mouth.

sprinkling back to my tongue.

I need to taste it

I need to know you can feel

the witchery gurgling inside of me.

I need to know that

I am the source of your agony.

And that which keeps

you up at night.

I need your thirst and your hunger.

I want to eat your despair for dinner.

As I crave you craving me

like a drug

you can never have enough of.

Shaking, sweating,

your hands desperate for my skin.

My love for you is obscene,

it crawls on the floor

where the impure things live.

So sign this paper with your blood

and give me your soul.

So I can entrap it

between my legs

so you can never escape.

so you're forever mine.

39

Today I don't want to think of things

that make me feel heavy or sad.

I don't want to feel the cold breeze

that travels through the Arctic.

again touching my face.

No.

today I don't want to remember

the nights I spent awake.

or

all the concerns

I have about existing...

Today I want to look

outside the window

and feel the warmth of the sun

bringing up the copper colour

of my hair.

warming up my cheeks
warming up my spirit.
Today I want to lie down
in white clean sheets
and drink kisses from your lips.
I want to look at you in the eye
and feel content.
Today I want you
to run your fingertips

along the bumps of my spine

and give me chills.

I don't want to play games.

wait for text messages

and feeds refreshing.

I don't want to look outside our minds.

our talks and our minutes in silence.

Today I just want to lose myself

in your heavy breath.

in your chest

rising and falling for me.

Today I want to be submerged

in a trance of sweat.

pleasure and laughter.

Today I want to smile for no reason.

I want to sleep soundly

and wake up in the middle of the day.

Rested. renewed

knowing you're there.

feet touching mine.

Today I don't care about you leaving

or about the future.

I don't want to feel

I have to prove myself

to be the best, to be the most...

I just want to be.

Today I want to drink coffee in

silence.

while we listen to our own heartbeats.

Playing the sweetest song

we could possibly grasp.

I want to smell the fragrance

of that coffee

coming from your breath

when we make love

Your strong hands on my hips.

eyes locked.

As the poet once said:

"I no longer need you to fuck me
as hard as I hated myself.
Make Love to me!"*
Today I just want some love
nothing else.

*(Part taken from the poem "We wer
emergencies" from the genius Buddy
(Wakefield)

40

People might not understand

why you are the way you are,

or why you do the things you do.

Their lack of understanding

won't determine

whether you are right or wrong.

Your path only belongs to you.

Your life only belongs to you.

You are the soul of a Goddess.

animating the beautiful vessel of flesh

that composes your being.

Be kind with it. Love it.

love what you are with pride.

chin up.

Wear your smile like

the perfect dress and go.

Life falls into place when you do that.

Trust me.

To all my sisters

41

I need the certainty that you are going
to look at me in the eye
and tell me I am wrong.
Even when I don't want to accept
or admit it.
I need you to wake me in the night.
tell me when it's time to give up
and there is no shame in it.

I need you to hug me

when I'm broken

and gather the cracked pieces

with gentle kisses.

I need you to leave me

when I am being unreasonable.

let me think about my mistakes

so I can call you back...

I need you to come back

to smile and tell me 'I told you so!'

I need you to be stubborn.

feet on the ground

when I am flying above reality.

I need objectivity

when my feelings get in the way.

for me to see things how they truly are.

I need protection from what I am.

from the tendency I have

to kill off the best parts of myself

every now and then.

I need someone to take

the poison glass

away from my hands

and give me hope instead.

so I can forget the stupid ideas

I always have in the middle

of cold nights.

When the silence feels more deadly
than anything else.
I need you to love me harder
when I least deserve it
because that's when I'll need it the
most.

42

The storm within

I woke up to the sound

of a hummingbird's wings

flapping close to my ears.

It was drinking the nectar

I normally let drip from my mind

when I sleep and dream of the future.

It told me the time was close
and I should prepare myself.
I knew the day would come
when I'd be ready to love again.
so I reached my hands to the cosmos
and waited.

The little bird whispered in my ear

that someone wearing cloudy shoes

and wings made of glitter

would come to me.

He'd be sweet and not scared

of the storm I have within.

but I should let just a little breeze

touch his face at first.

It told me I should close my eyes.

so I could truly see.

told me to stop looking for things.

so I could find them.

told me stillness is only found

within chaos —

and only now

that my love for myself was complete

could I share it

with another human being.

So I believed it.

I gathered the last pink flowers

I was cultivating in between my

breasts.

took their petals off.

whispered an incantation to them

on my palms

and blew them away

into the starry night.

They flew around in circles

taking the hummingbird's predictions

and the warmth of my breath

with them.

taking the hope and the faith

that there, somewhere

submerged in the darkness

of the celestial sphere

    someone was also waiting for m

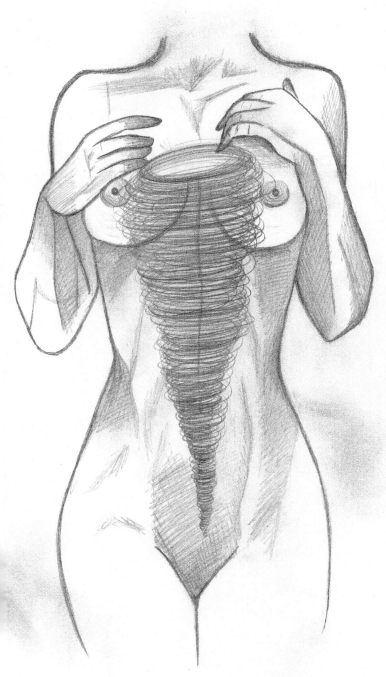

237

43

You look at me, but you don't see me.

You hear my voice,

but you can't listen to the truth.

You see my bare skin, naked

but you cannot see what's under it.

My voice echoes something

that you might

think as shallow and superficial.

but my music goes deeper, further.

Few can feel the warmth of my words,

the purity of my intentions

and the size of the dreams

I project in the sky.

Don't judge me

for some random words,

don't take me for granted.

Don't think I am floating around

like a lost kite.

Defining and labelling
is a mistake many made.
The marks on my skin
are more profound
than you can possibly imagine,
and my tears made a pool
you could drown in.
But choosing to look only at this
you lose out on the sunlight
hidden behind my eyelids.

the astonishing rainbow

I have resting

in the back on my neck.

and the golden pot of honey

I have resting under my tongue.

See me for who I am.

44

I am Sorry

I wish I could start this one

with a little less weight

pushing down my shoulders.

I don't want to feel

the heavy hands of guilt

tightening around my neck anymore.

I wish I could go back in time

to fix past mistakes, wrong paths

and irrational decisions

so things would be a bit easier,

a bit lighter.

With my knees on the ground,

my heart in my hands,

and dressed up only in honesty

I came all this way to apologise.

I am sorry for all the times

       I couldn't be a good friend.

for the times I was not there for you

      when you needed me.

Maybe because I was absorbed

      in my own traffic jams

Maybe because I was being careless

      Or maybe even because

I couldn't reach out enough

      to understand your sorrows —

for the times I couldn't

be patient enough

to kiss your scars

and listen to the music

your tears were singing.

I am sorry for the times

I betrayed your trust

and cut up the thin skin of your faith

in me

I am sorry!

I'm sorry I couldn't be a good
daughter, a good sister.
Being part of a broken family
was too painful to deal.
I should have been there for you,
crying and laughing with you,
fighting our struggles together,
facing the tornados with our faces up,
hands held tight
like family does.

I am sorry!

I'm sorry that sometimes

I couldn't be a good lover.

a good girlfriend.

Letting someone

get this close to my essence

So they can hear my heart beat

always petrified me.

And the few times it happened

I might have freaked out.

might have acted out.

might have been odd and out of myself.

I'm sorry I scared you

sometimes with too much passion.

sometimes with too little.

I'm sorry I couldn't stay

when you needed me.

that I couldn't take care of your heart.

when you placed it

so carefully in my palms.

I am sorry

to all of you —

all loved ones, forgotten ones,

Dead ones.

I might not be an ideal person,

but I'm trying.

I'm working on the pile

of bad decisions

I have been collecting over the years,

and it's a big one.

I just want you to know

that I am aware.

I am awake and I am trying.

I am sorry!

45

The maze

Today my eyes gazed through the
translucent glass of the train window.
the world outside gazed back at me
and spoke with my core without words.
Seeing the trees and the cotton clouds.

pass by

so fast.

I saw how life and dreams

can also pass by

right in front of our eyes.

I came to realise

we all live in a maze.

We don't all cross the same labyrinth,

but they all take us to the same

destination.

We walk in circles,

confuse directions.

start over.

feel lost and sometimes give up.

We hit our faces at walls

and heaven seems too far away

Just few can understand

it's never about the end

It's all about the path.

it always has been.

the roads you're going to cross

and the ones you meet along the way.

I figured the water founts

we drink from

and the stones we face.

are the crucial parts —

how they make you stronger.

making you trip over your feet.

and how each fall brings

wisdom and valuable lessons.

The end of the maze is to face death.

It only matters how you got there,

looking back,

with happy and content eyes,

knowing it was all worth it.

All the efforts, the losses,

nights spent awake and the laughter,

the smiles of loved ones,

hugs and tears under the rain,

the pain and suffering.

To know that

in the end

there was light

living within yourself all along

and you were able to find it.

enjoy it.

spread it on the ground

to pave the roads for the ones

coming after you.

46 – (The first and the last)

Who Am I?

I am the twilight

and the dawn you don't see.

I am the sky with no stars

and the moonlight.

hidden by those sad clouds.

I am the humming bird's wings

flapping in the air, almost invisible

and buzzing.

I am the winter fog.

creeping into your garden.

slowly and in silence.

making everything around still

and white.

I am your latest tear.

the last one

when the pain just settles in

and the suffering is finally gone.

I am the desire to be and stay,

and the will to go

with no destination, no end.

I am the alcoholic torrent

circulating your veins,

inebriating your thoughts,

and confusing your senses.

I am the burning desire

that ignites you when you love

and feel pleasure.
I am the flame burning in your eyes
and your skin when you dream.
I am the winter breeze,
blowing your hair
and causing chills
to go up your spine.
I am the music playing
when you dance and get drunk

I am your intoxication.

And the noise tormenting your soul!

The end

but not quite.

This is it – you made it to the end.

Now you have my soul.

Placed gently in your palms.

so pass it along. ~~It~~ belongs to you now.

Give it to the ones you feel deserve.

want, or need it.

so more people can enjoy the words I

planted

so carefully

in these pages,

and with so much love.

It's yours to decide.

I hope it spoke to you

I hope it touched you

I hope you feel better after all

I hope you felt things,

no matter what they were.

Thank you for helping fulfilling my call!

Mariana Prado

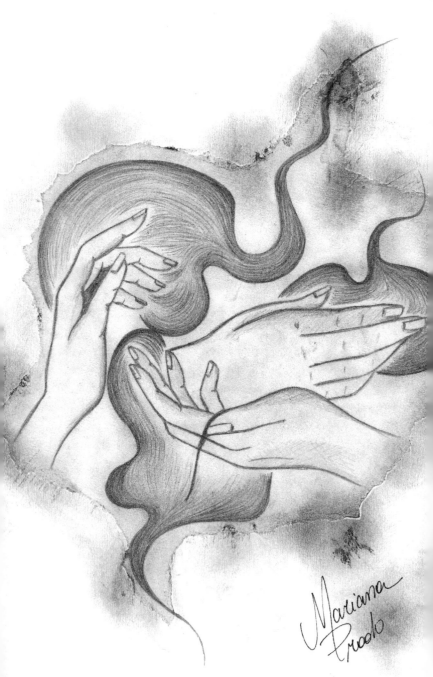

Mariana
Prooß

Printed in Great Britain
by Amazon